The Number Five

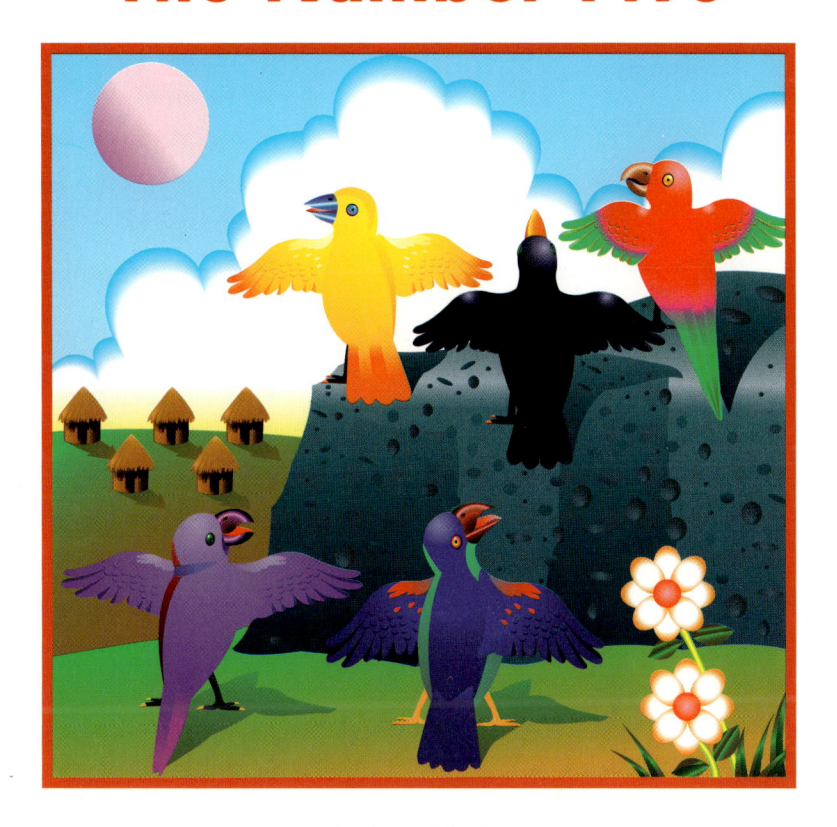

Adria Klein
Illustrated by Yemi

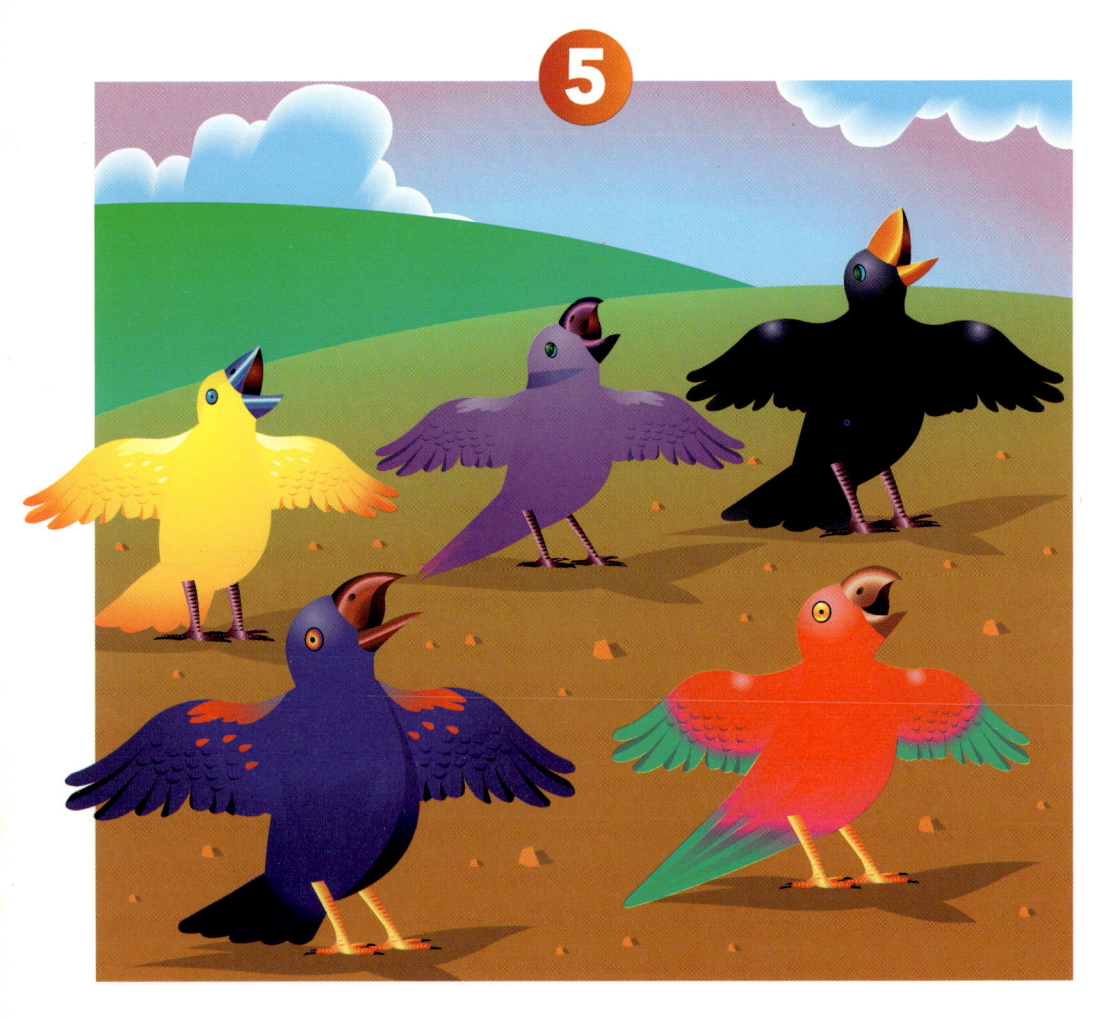

Five big birds sing

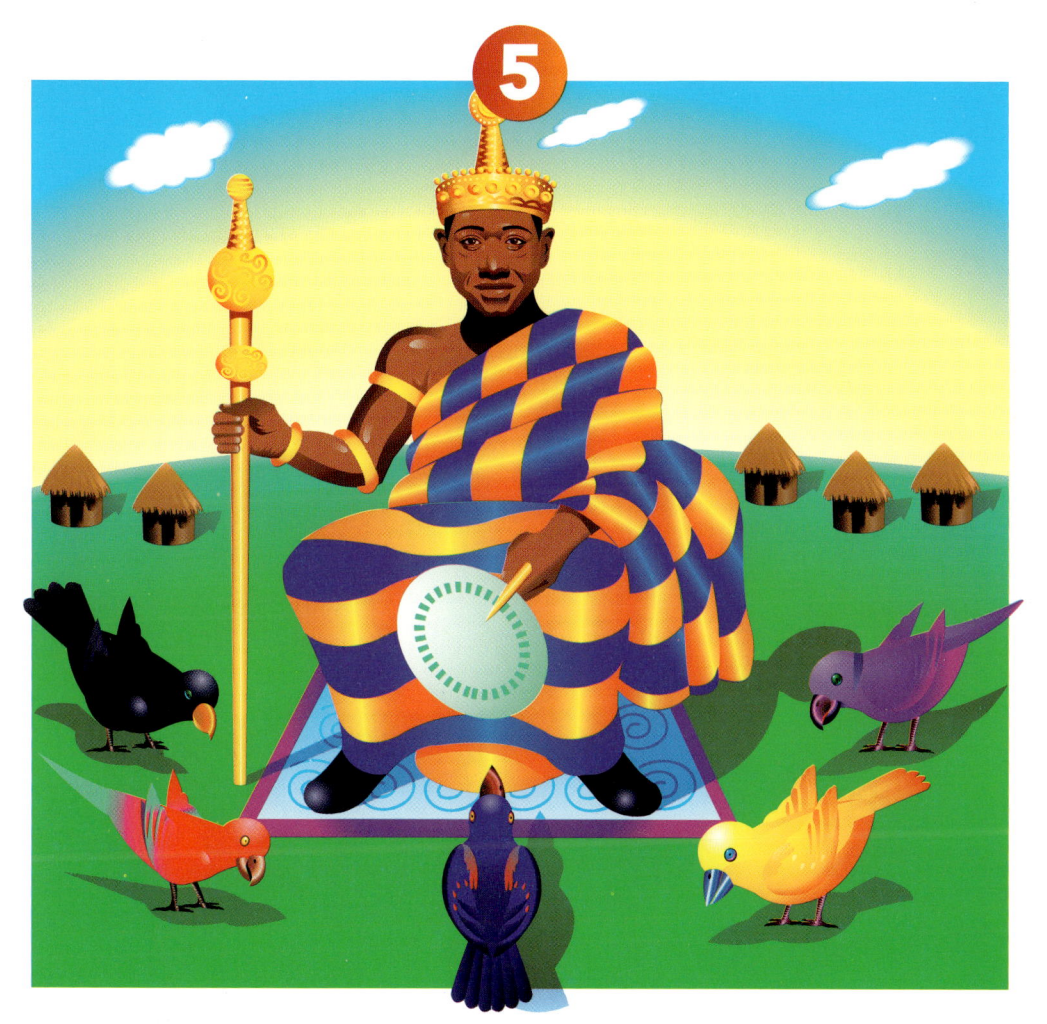

and bow to the king.

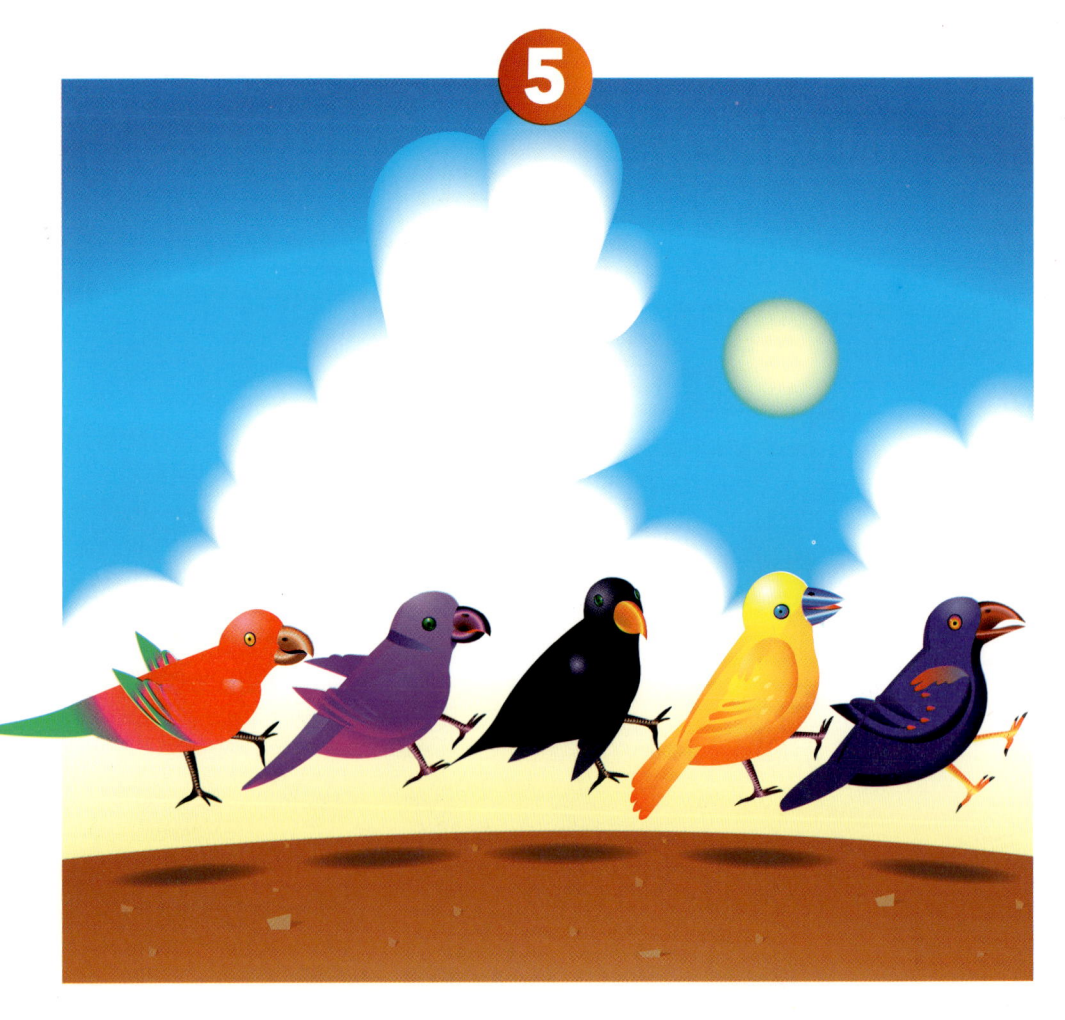

Five big birds hop

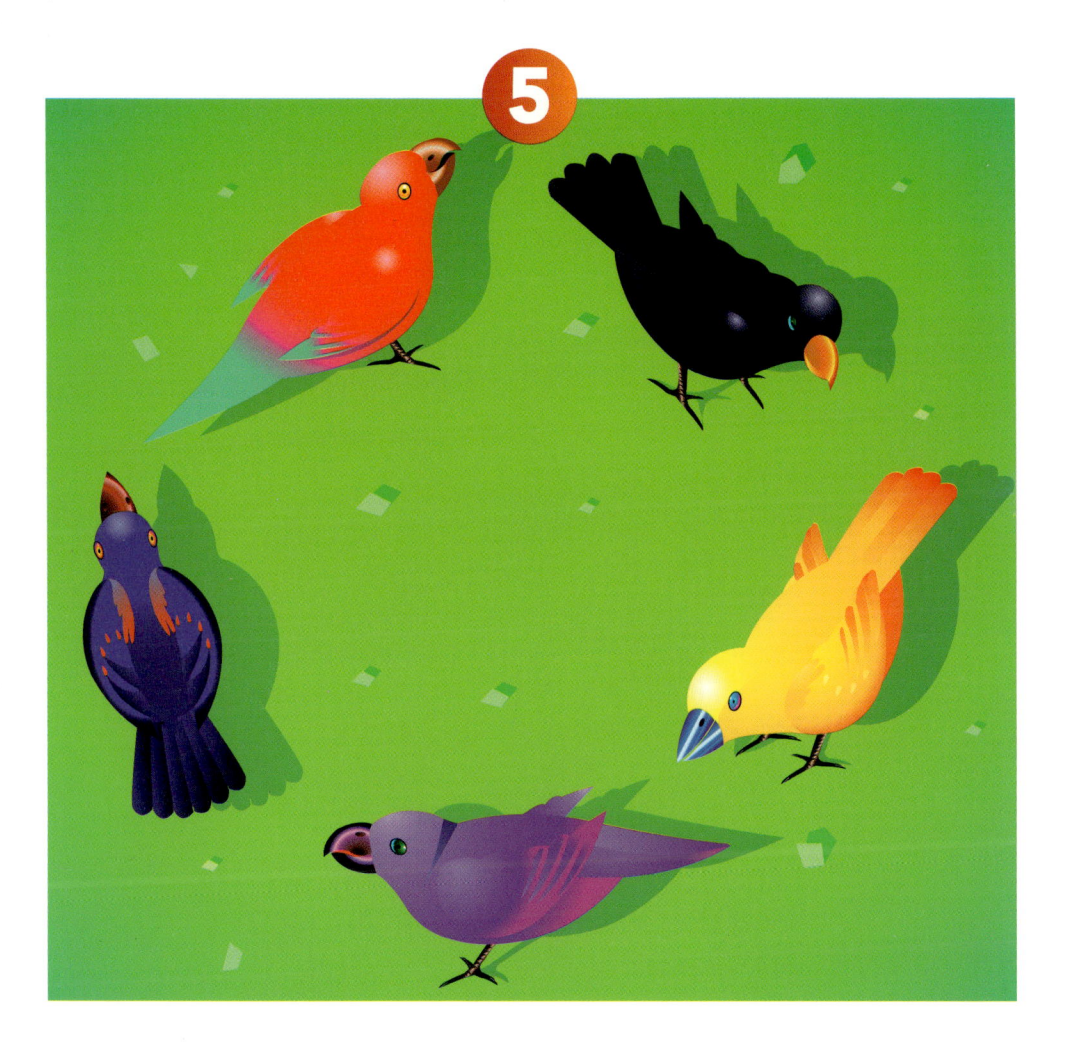

and turn like a top.

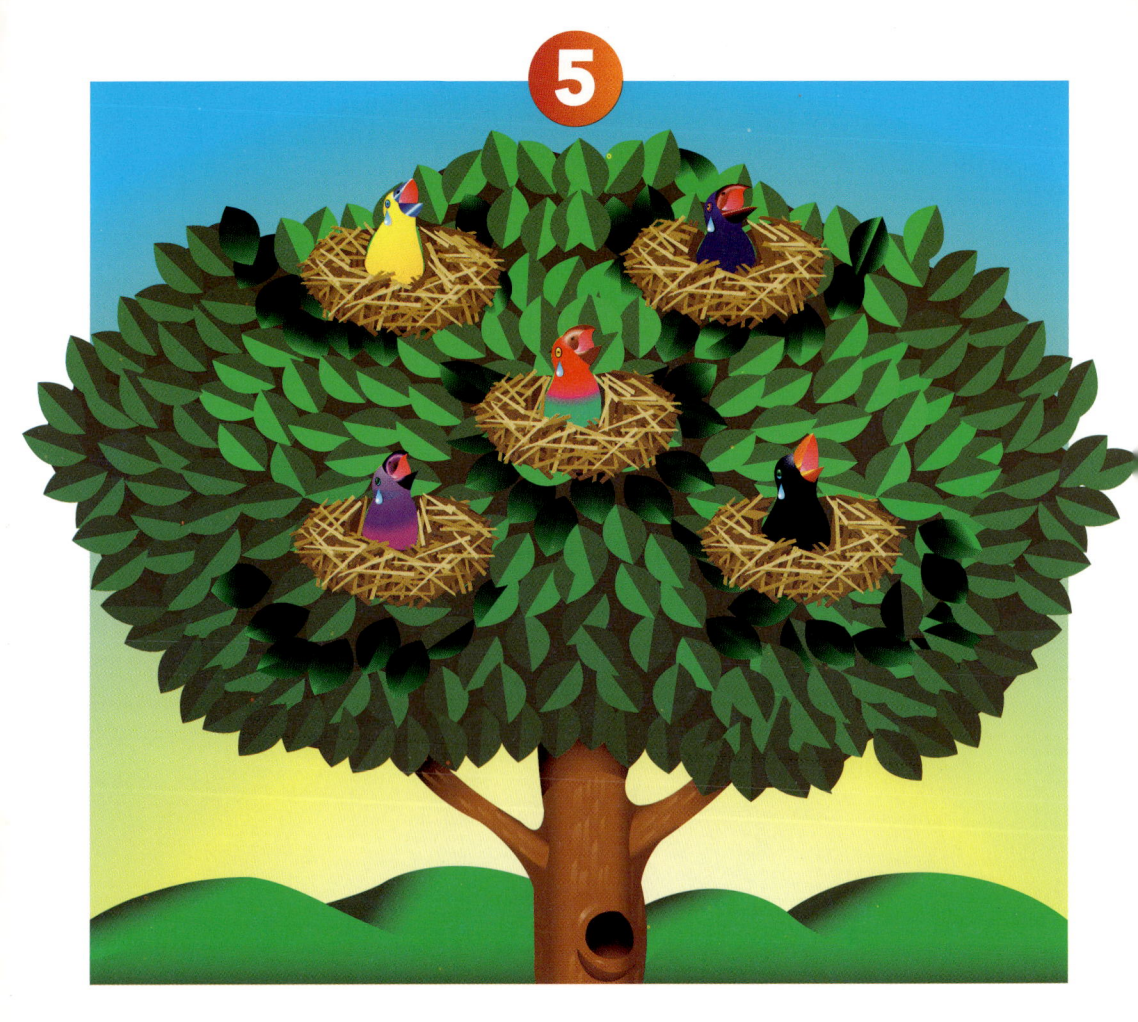

Five baby birds cry.

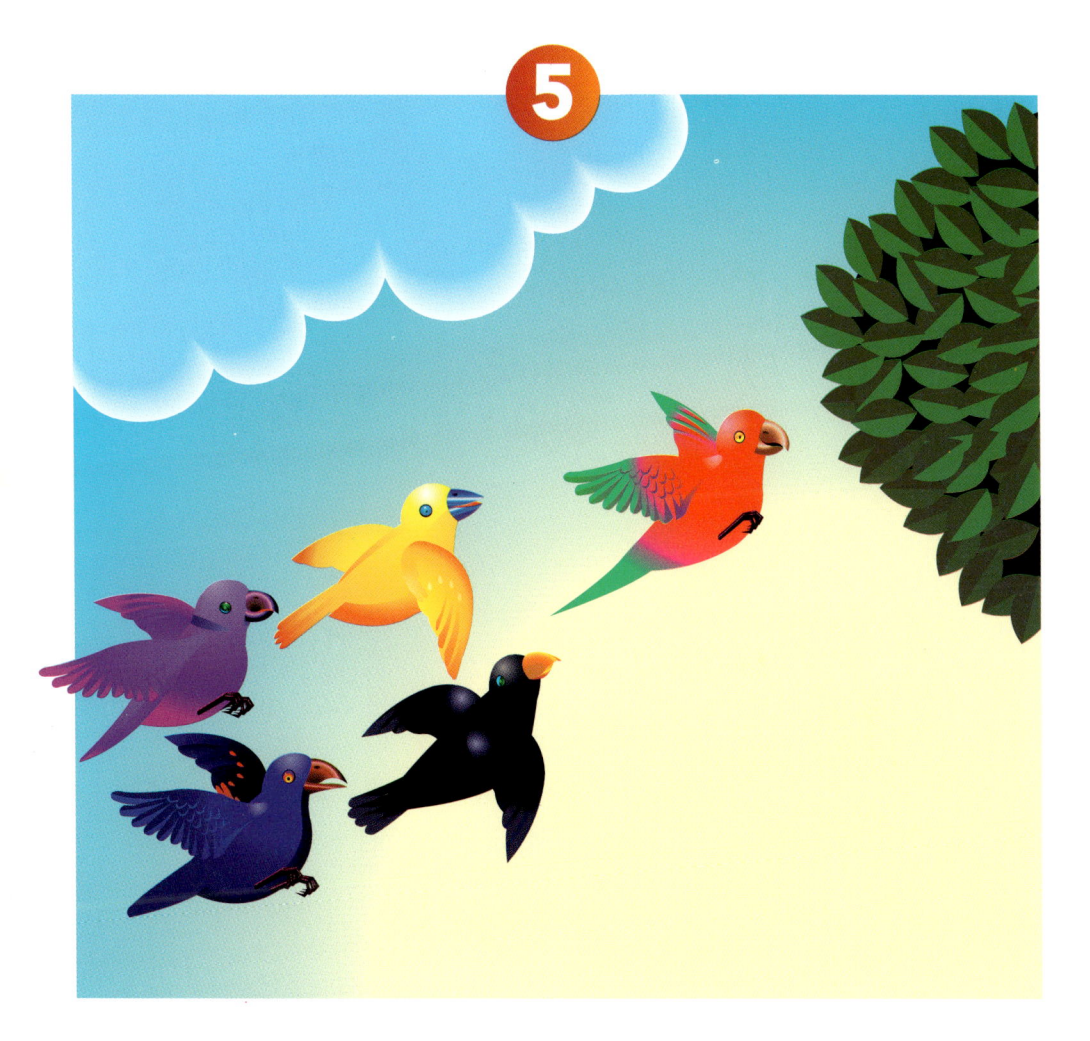

Five big birds fly high.

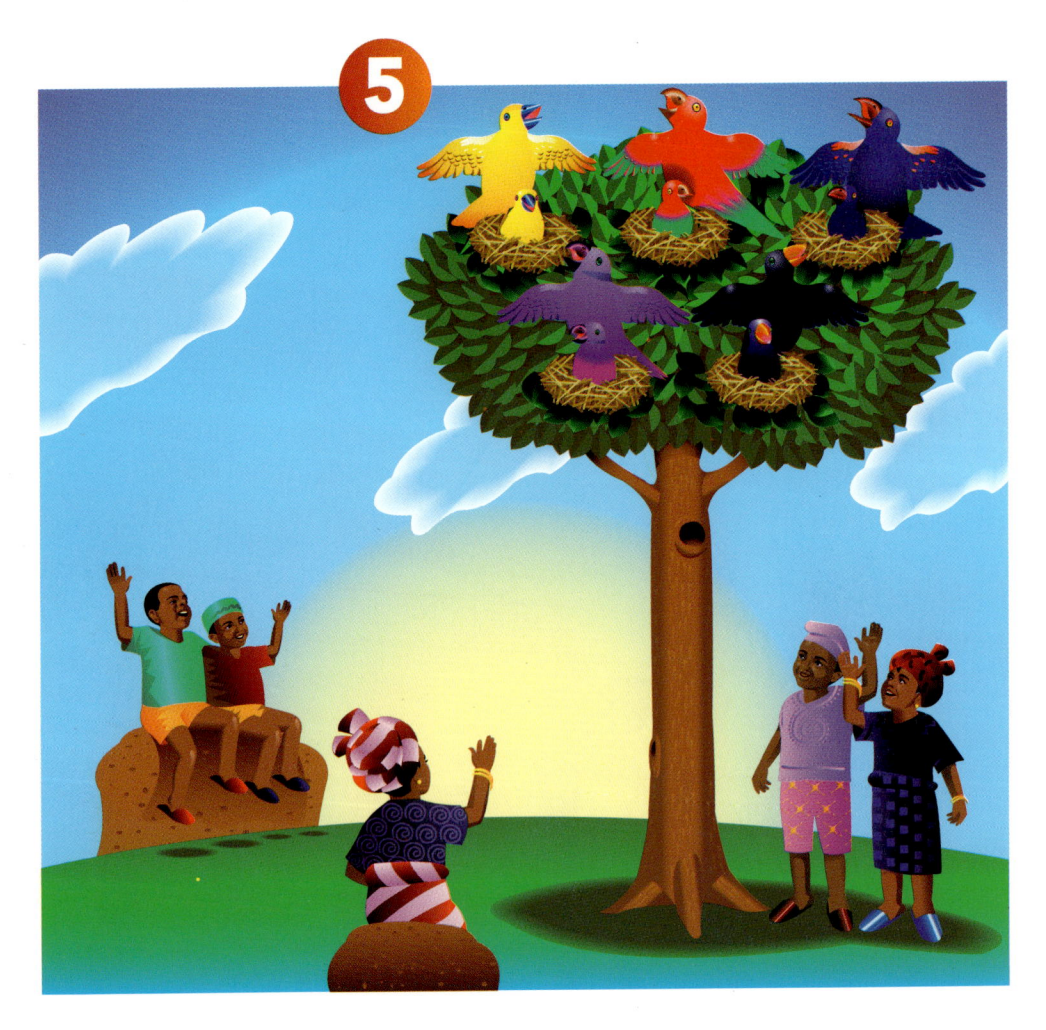

Five children wave goodbye.